THE CIRCLE OF LOVE

Debashis Chatterjee is currently Professor of Organisation Behaviour at the Indian Institute of Management, Lucknow where he heads a global centre for Leadership and Human Values. He has also taught at Harvard University as Senior Fulbright Professor. Author of *Leading Consciously* and *Light the Fire in Your Heart,* he has been a trainer in several Fortune 100 corporations and has taken his inspirational message to all six continents of the world.

The Circle of Love is his first book of fiction in free verse. He can be reached at www.debchat.com.

THE CIRCLE OF LOVE

Debashis Chatterjee

To Baba

Love & Regards!

Debashis

Rupa & Co

To My Circle ...

Aditi, Anoop, Ajit, Linda, Brad, Bridget, Jenny, Martyn, Aruna, Laurel, Bernie, Annamia, Anu, Kanchan, Haimanti, Chandan, Shona, Atul, Chander Prakash, Vandana, Narayana, Svenja, Sharon, Saikat, Nena, Marianne, Mukund, Shrishti, Suzanne, Soumenda, Vivek, Roli, Parimal, Sanjoy, Pritam, Siddharth, Uttamda, Jayabroto, Sujata, Saurav, Amrita, Dominic, Diya, Anirban, Shabasana, Dawn and Jennie

Published 2005 by
Rupa & Co
7/16, Ansari Road, Daryaganj,
New Delhi 110 002

Sales Centres:
Allahabad Bangalore Chandigarh
Chennai Hyderabad Jaipur Kathmandu
Kolkata Mumbai Pune

Typeset in 12 pt. Hiroshige by Nikita Overseas Pvt Ltd
1410 Chiranjiv Tower, 43 Nehru Place, New Delhi 110 019

Printed in India by Saurabh Printers Pvt Ltd,
A-16, Sector-IV, Noida 201 301

Contents

Preface

To call this, *The Return of the Prophet*
would be pompous or sheer blasphemy
for, has the Prophet ever left us to
interminably wait?
The poet's heart stirred in me
love's new alchemy.
His spirit lifted me, moved and muted me
near river Charles, close to Harvard Square,
while shuffling through tedious reports
amidst a noisy church choir.
For nature, my teacher, taught me with a
gusto,
what I never learnt from any management
manifesto.
I learnt that birds fly as they have faith in
their wings,
but, bards fly on the wings of faith,
yours truly thinks.
I would have called this *Nature's Manuscript*

so that it sounds more poetic or even discreet.
But Love had its way, saying I trespass everywhere,
my centre is at the heart of every lover and my fence nowhere.
So complete this Circle, Dear Reader, in joy, not as a chore,
for I lived and loved many moments writing this, for you to adore.
The words explore the path of love,
both human and divine,
the credit goes to Gibran,
the blemishes are mine.

Forget not that I shall come back to you.
A little while, and my longing shall gather dust
and foam for another body.
A little while, a moment of rest upon the wind,
and another woman shall bear me.

KAHLIL GIBRAN

The world removes its mask of
vastness to its lover.

RABINDRANATH TAGORE

The Circle of Love

The sun turned lavender, mauve, then red
in Rishikesh.
The sky looked a strange painting,
as though a playful child
had spilled blobs of paint on blue canvas.
Far away, bells rang in hypnotic harmony.
And Ganga curled on luminous round stones
in passionate embrace.

A temple stood wrapped in the mystery of the
mountains.
Its stairs full
with smell of camphor and marigolds.
Devotees sat solemn faced, waiting for
Ananda to speak —
eyes expectant like parched earth.
Seekers of truth swayed to the sound of
cymbals …
blonde, brunette and bald heads swung
in unspeakable ecstasy.

In the distance, two children giggled away
blissfully lost in their world,
their laughter made more audible by the
welcoming wind.
Their voices rang like beads
rolling on marble floor.

Mariann sat gazing into Ananda's
still, soulful eyes.
He sat straight like an exquisite work of art,
his face soft and unmasked
without a ripple of sorrow.
The sun shone in his eyes in a speck of stardust.
When Ananda smiled, Mariann's heart lit up
in the surge of a magnificent moment.
She whispered to a woman sitting by her:
He appears like a man
living between dream and reality.
The woman nodded:
Honestly, I think he is a messenger
from an unnamed star.

For Mariann, life in Rishikesh seemed like a
fairytale,

far from the haze of streetlights in downtown
Boston.
There, unseasonal rain
would fill the mind with strange emotions.
She would soak herself
like a school-sick child
soul-deep in troubled waters
as she hurried to catch the outbound metro.

Here, in Rishikesh,
was all the time to watch a palm leaf boat
glide through the river swelling like a belly,
stirring currents in her heart too deep to
fathom.

For one thing, spring was here.
A pair of lovers cuddled like charmed snakes.
And the riot of bees made the magic of the
evening even more magical.

Mariann thought,
it seems ages since
I have been in love like this.
Her slender hand coursed through her hair,
lush and golden as a ripe paddy field.
Her eyes sparkled like crystals struck by light,

a wave of joy crept through her body.
Her mind was lucid as a freshly sprouted leaf.

Ananda's voice, clear and crisp, pierced the ears of his listeners
like the rapture of wind rustling through bamboo leaves.
He said, Listen! What I say to you is
as old as the rocks:
Every child born is a living proof
that existence is not tired of its creation.

Ananda paused.
Temple bells have now fallen silent.
The music has stopped.
Evening has begun to fold itself up
in the comforting lap of night.

He continued:
Love is a man in quest for the child within,
a woman longing for the fountain of life,
a saint's search for the Self,
a traveller's lust for the world.
Love is our freedom song.

The river finds freedom in its flow,
the flower in its blooming,
the swallow in its flight,
and gold in its glow.
We all find freedom in love.

Love is the heart of our freedom.
Love is the source of all that is free-flowing.
Yet we cannot see love just as we cannot see
freedom;
we can merely see their trailing shadows.
You may collect all the petals of a rose
yet you cannot gather its beauty.
You may hold all the water of the river yet
never find its flow.
You may cage a swallow
yet not arrest its song.

Love drives the golden chariot of spring —
its unseen hand creating a million names and
forms
from the heart of one life,
scattering them with abandon
like mustard seeds.

Circle of Love

Love is a man in quest for the child within.
A woman longing for the fountain of life.
A saint's search for the self.
A traveller's lust for the world

Love is our freedom song
The river finds freedom in its flow.
The flower finds freedom in its blooming
The swallow finds freedom in its flight.
And gold finds freedom in its glow.
We all find freedom in love.

Yet we cannot see love just as we cannot see freedom;
We can merely see their trailing shadows.
You may collect all the petals of a rose
yet you cannot gather its beauty.
You may hold all the water of the river yet never find its flow.
You may cage a swallow
yet not arrest its song.

Omnipresent yet invisible,
standing still while spanning the universe.
There is no way to love,
for love is the only way:
all that it creates in the world,
return to their source
in one grand circle of life.

Mariann asked: With what tools does love create?
Ananda replied:
Love creates by holding a dream within itself
as firmly as a sculptor holds a chisel
in his hand.
In our imagination are love's fertile forms.
These forms become real when
our dreams find fuel in the desire of our heart.
All of creation moves
in the circle of love.

On Creation

Mariann's smile lingered like a
whiff of oriental perfume
slowly suffusing her face.
The day was breaking through the vastness of
a banyan tree
in searching, sensuous spirals of light.
She said,
Tell us about Creation.

Ananda spoke.
His voice fell like dewdrops
on a hushed field
stretched like a mesmerised lover.

First, there was the joy of the One that was
born of itself.
It was both luminous and conscious.
Its nature was bliss, knowledge and
truth absolute.

Being self-aware but lonely
the One decided to play with its own light.

Like a prism of crystal that scatters one light in
many colours,
the One born of itself scattered its own
luminous
essence in man and woman.

The point of light within a man was being,
and the flame born of this light within a
woman was becoming.
They were different yet inseparable from each
other like fire and heat.

This being and becoming were held together
by three silken threads:
the thread of desire,
of knowledge,
of creation.
Through the power of desire
man and woman longed for each other
in the garden of being and becoming.

On Creation

ke a prism of crystal that scatters one
ght in many colours
e One born of itself scattered its own
uminous essence in a man and a woman.

e point of light inside a man was being;
nd the flame born of this light inside a
oman was becoming.
ey were different yet inseparable from
ach other
ke fire and heat.

is being and becoming were held together
y three silken threads:
e thread of desire,
Knowledge,
creation.

rough the power of desire
man and a woman longed for each other
n the garden of being and becoming.
rough Knowledge
y became curious to discover each other
ven as they were two limbs of the body of One.
rough creation a man and a woman filled
e universe of One with many names and forms.

Through knowledge
they became curious to discover each other
even as they were two limbs
of the One body.
Through creation man and woman filled
the universe of One with many names and
forms.

Mariann asked,
If we are all born of the One
why is it that we experience ourselves as
different?

Ananda said:
Because of the way we use our three powers.
We limit the power of knowledge by seeking
our selves in the world of differences
rather than in the unity within us.
We limit desire by craving
trifles that draw us away from our
inborn wholeness.
We limit creation by chasing shadows cast
against our luminous essence,
which is bliss, knowledge and truth absolute.

On Bondage

Mariann looked at the lurking, inky clouds
rumbling in the distant horizon.
The silken arches of her brow curved
like folded wings —
a flash of fear in her eyes.
She asked,
How does the One that is forever free get
chained?

Said Ananda, his voice smooth
as the silent breath of the night:
The One who is always free
is bound in Time, Space and Causation.

The traveller of Eternity becomes
a prisoner of the mind's conception of time as
past and future.
Thus bound in time he divides his life in many
anxious moments
when he should fill them with One eternal life.

On Bondage

The One who is always free
is bound in Time, Space and Causation.

The traveller of Eternity becomes
a prisoner of the mind's conception of time
as past and future.
Thus bound in time he divides his life
many anxious moments
When he shoul fill all his moments
with One eternal life.
He then falls from the fetterless grace of life
into a prison made of memory and desire.

The One unbounded is confined in space
inside the house of skin and bone.
Guarded by the five senses and enslaved
by five elements
his bondage is a prison of his own making
while the essence in him flutters like
a bird trapped in cage.

Finally, the one becomes a prisoner of causation.
He begins to see himself as a procession of matter
and mind;
and forgets that matter is just a shape
and mind just a name
He gives to his nameless and formless essence.

He then falls from the unfettered grace of life
into a prison of past memory and desire for
the future.
The One who inhabits all that there is
thus becomes bound in space.
The One unbounded, is confined
within skin and bone.
Guarded by the senses and enslaved by five
elements,
he is bound in the prison of his own making
while the essence in him flutters
like a caged bird.

Finally, the One becomes a prisoner of
causation.
He begins to see himself as a procession of
mind and matter;
and forgets that matter is just a shape and
mind merely a name
he gives to his nameless and formless essence.
He sees his being as a temporary succession
of events rather than
one uncaused and timeless tide.

The One born free is thus bound in chains.

On Space

In the misty morning
the pilgrims
wound their way up the mountain.
The sun winked its wondrous presence
through a swirl of cloud.
The birds heralded a new dawn.
Ananda sat with eyes transfixed
on the green-grey mountain top
peeping through the mist.
The pilgrims sat in that enchanted space.

The builder of houses then asked,
Tell us about Space.

Ananda's eyes swept the vast mountains as
he said:
The house that you build is a mere ornament
for space.
We are all housed in space.

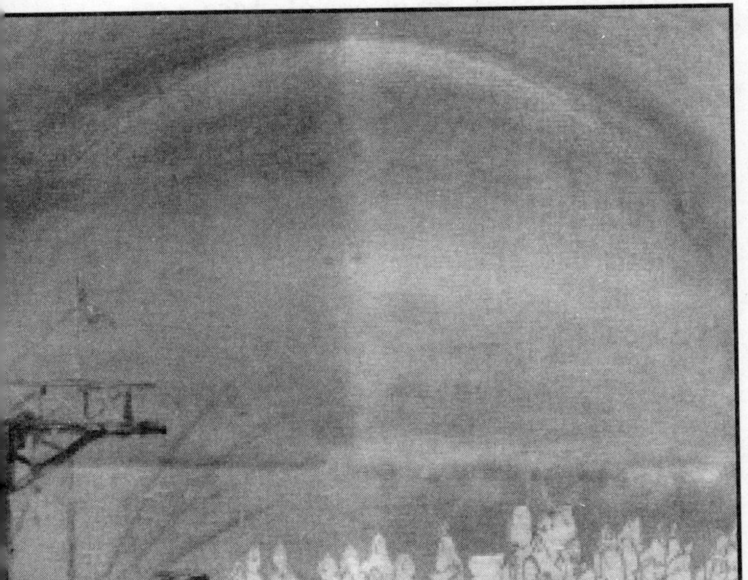

Our bodies are mansions of space
with nine doors.
Our senses are like fences around this mansion.
Our desires are but forms of enclosed space.
Through many desires our minds shape space
so that it can count the world of the One as many.

Everything that you can see, touch, hear or feel is in space.
For space simply is.
The only gift you can give your beloved
is the gift of space.
It is the ultimate wealth.
In unbounded space we find our true abundance,
just as the sweeping eagle discovers its omnipresence
in the freedom of the sky.

Space is not a gulf between walls
and objects —
it is our true nature.

Our thoughts, like our walls, hold our space
in ransom.
Brick by brick you shape your house;
thought by thought you shape the space in
your body.
To enter the space within your bodies
you must look behind the veil of thoughts
into your original nature which is thoughtless
space.

Space is relationship without resistance.
Space is shared silence unbroken by a ripple
of thought.
It is the ultimate ground of togetherness.
In true kinship we discover the seamless space
that contains us.
Space is growth, unbounded life of
prosperity.
The wild flower grows in space as it is visited
by the bee.
For the flower the bee is not an unwelcome
intruder
but a companion in space.

The bee proclaims the message of a single
flower to an entire forest;
in relationship we reclaim our infinite spaces.

The space within is the same as the space
without.
You limit your space as you narrow your
horizon
by dropping your eyelashes
while face to face with the blazing sun.

Just as the outer space is filled with
smoke, dust and dirt,
with anger, greed and lust for power
you poison your inner space.

Your life's aspiration is merely to quench its
thirst for space.
The potter thinks he moulds clay for eternity,
yet, he merely surrounds space with a mortal
frame.
Our physical life is no more than a clay pot
that reaches out of the master potter's hands
before bowing down to the dust of His feet.

On Space

e only gift that you can give to your beloved
the gift of space.
is gift is the ultimate wealth
n unbounded space we find our true abundance
st as a sweeping eagle discovers its omnipresence
the freedom of the sky.

pace is relationship without resistance.
t is the ultimate ground of togetherness.
n true Kinship we discover the seemless
pace that contains us

pace is growth; unbounded life of prosperity.
e wild flower grows in space as it is
sited by the bee.
r the flower the bee is not an unwelcome
truder
ut a companion in space.
he bee proclaims the message of a single
lower to an entire forest.
n relationship we reclaim our vaster spaces

Be not a trader is space.
For how can you trade that which is the essence of all,
and therefore, the presence in all.
Offer space as though you offer yourself.
Your reward will be
the vast expanse of the sky
and the calm depths of the ocean.

Saying this, Ananda looked at a blue mountain bird
swooping down against the sun.
Its glittering wings caught the sun's rays and soared with the wind.
A creature of space —
it glided through the sky,
leaving no trace of its flight.

On Time

An old watchmaker looked warily at the
speeding day.
Nature had imprinted its solemn parting song
on his deeply lined face — a fortress in ruins.

He asked,
Tell us about Time.

Ananda spoke:
Time is not like a mountain path,
a winding thread from here to eternity.
Time is a room full unto itself.
All of time is here in this room.
Like a magical cobweb
time spreads its wings from the womb
of here and now
and curves back to itself
at the end of a life's span.

Here in this room is all that is present in time
past.
Although you may look
into the distant future,
the one looking still occupies the room.
It is from this now-here that all of our past
and future grow.

There are three kinds of time.
First, what the clock shows us.
The hands of the clock are like
a feverish beloved
waiting interminably for her lover.
Stung by her wavering passion
she jumps from the past to the future,
never staying in the moment.
The time of the clock recedes from her forever
like her own shadow —
an elusive bubble of hope and despair.
And like her shadow, it is unreal.

There is another kind of time,
circular in nature —
the time of the four seasons.

On Time

Then, an old watchmaker looked warily
at the speeding day.
Nature had imprinted its solemn parting song
on his deeply lined face – a fortress in ruins.

He asked,
Tell us about the Time.

Ananda spoke:
Time is not like a mountain path,
a winding thread from here to eternity
Time is a room that is full unto itself.
All of Time is here in this room.

Like a magical cobweb
Time spreads its wings from
the womb of now and here
and curves back to itself
at the end of a life's span.

Here in this room is all that is present in time
past.
Although you may look out of the room
into the distant future,
the one looking still occupies the room.
It is from this now-here that all of our past
and future grow.

Like a wheel, this time
turns away, yet returns
in never ending cycles
like the wheel of spring and summer,
of death and resurrection.
From this circular time is created
all of nature's fertile forms:
all that move and grow, cry or crawl,
roar and run.
In this time
the anxious maiden becomes a mother.

There is a third kind of time —
the time of our mind.
Sprouting like a seed,
it grows as we feel joy,
it shrinks as we feel fear.
In the mind's time
the mother becomes the sorceress.
She beguiles us with her measures and magic.
Time becomes short and long, dark and light,
sad and happy.

Finally, the source of time
is the timeless.
In the timeless,
the sorceress becomes the seer.
As she looks through the veil of time
she uncovers that eternity
where time stands still.

On Desire

As Mariann spoke,
the wind caressed her billowing blouse.
Like ivy, her infinite longing climbed
with the rising of each breath —
eager to feel every secret of her body.
Her hair was blown apart like a scattered flame
with lustrous tongues probing the night's mystery;
her cheek glowed like an oyster shell.

She said, Tell us of Desire.

Ananda spoke:
Desire is the first born in our nature —
the seed from which we emerge.
The root of all desire is the desire for life.

All desires spread like branches from that one desire to live.

Every flicker of desire is a search for the flame of the living Self.
All desires emerge from and merge into the Self.
Just as every ray of light comes from the Sun and dissolves into the Sun.

The world is a creation of desire.
A flickering flame can set a whole city on fire;
a little seed of desire can fill the world with myriad shapes and forms.
All that is brought to life is nothing but the fruit of desire.

Desire is also born in Time and dissolves in Time.
There can be no desire without past and future.
In the present, there is no desire.
Tied to the memory of the past,
the horse of desire speeds on the road of hope, of future.
It is a prisoner of memory and hope.

Therefore, know that all desiring is a journey away from our Self,

like the skin of an apple is far removed from
its core.
The real essence of the apple lies in its taste.

This taste lies not in the apple but in our
experience of this taste.
The skin is merely a bait to rouse our desire
for taste.
The nature of taste, which I call the essence of
the apple, is in the depth of our Self.
Know that the sweetness we find in the apple
is in our Self.
All that we crave for is in our Self.
Quivering desire merely creates an image of
our Self
in the many objects of the universe,
like the river's rippling water
creating illusion of many moons on its bosom.

Desiring is a never-ending caravan
crawling toward the dreary sands of nowhere.
The simmering desire for flesh, fortune or fame
is a receding oasis of illusion where the One
cannot truly rest.

On Desire

Desire is the first born in our nature.
It is the seed from which we emerge.
The root of all desire is the desire for life.

All other desires spread like branches
from that one desire to live.

Every flicker of desire is a search for the
flame of the living Self.
All desires emerge from and merge into
the Self.
Just as every ray of light comes from the
Sun
and dissolves into the Sun.

The world is a creation of desire.
A flickering flame can set a whole city on
fire.
A little seed of desire can fill the world
with myriad shapes and forms.
All that is brought to life is nothing
but the fruit of desire.

... desire to be desireless
like a blazing fire that writes its own obituary
in an ember's dying incandescence.

For what we truly desire is now and here.
We who cling to no particular house can be
at home everywhere.
We who need no hope can count every
moment as hopeful benediction.
The core of all desire is desirelessness —
the true nature of our Self.

There is a feverishness in the way
we pursue the object of our desire.
And after its consummation
we exclaim in joy.
Know for sure, this joy comes not from the
object you desire
but from that sacred space within where
all desires get fulfilled.
Be as spacious as the ocean that contains
all the ebbs and tides of desire
and is yet still in its depth.
This space is what I call desirelessness which
resides in the utmost depth of our Self.
So desire to be desireless like a blazing fire
that writes its own obituary
in an ember's dying incandescence.

On Play

Then a child arched like a question mark
against a tree said,
Sir, speak to us of Play.

And Ananda, his face breaking into a half
smile answered:
Play is the only meaning of life,
the only living philosophy.

You ask, why does the breeze blow?
Why do flowers bloom?
Why do autumn leaves wither and fall?
They do so because they are in play.
They do so because they are secured in their
own nature
even as they play.
For play is not the means to reach a higher
heaven.
Play is its own cause and justification.

On Play

Play is the only meaning of life
It is the only living philosophy.

In play we extend ourselves
like the sweep of the sea in high tide.
Then slowly we recede to ourselves.
Like the ebb and flow of water we see our
many manifestations.

A child becomes the whole universe as he
forgets himself in play.
It is here that he reclaims his
Omnipresent Self.

We who are no longer children in years,
mistake play as merely a retreat
from everyday drudgery
and not the mainstream of life.

For we do not know that in the
larger and ampler intelligence of life
we are the player as well as the play.

The joy in play is
the joy of wonder and self-discovery.
This is the joy of life itself.
Life is like the cycle of seasons —
it goes round and curves back on itself.
Spring comes and goes away,
only to return in a fiesta of flowers and leaves.

In play we extend ourselves
like the sweep of the sea in high tide.
Then slowly we recede to ourselves.
Like the ebb and flow of water we see our
many manifestations.
A child becomes the whole universe as he
forgets himself in play —
it is here that he reclaims his omnipresent Self.

We who are no longer children in years,
mistake play as merely a retreat
from everyday drudgery
and not the mainstream of life.
For we do not know that in the
greater intelligence of life
we are the player as well as the play.

On the Body

The physician said,
Speak to us about the Body.

Ananda spoke:
The body is a melody of five elements —
air, water, earth, fire and space.
It is the string on which
the music of the spirit is struck.
This eternal music floats in the air
and vanishes in time,
only to leave behind some fireside stories
that people remember at times.

Your body is a house of shadows
hiding the light of your spirit.
It is a road that stretches a lifetime
toward the island of the unknown.
Nay, the body is a lantern of knowledge.
When we clean its dusty walls,
the dwelling light is revealed.

There are many bodies within our body.
It is a battlefield of passion and dispassion.
The body of anger sizzles like a flame.
The body of understanding cools it.
The body of fear recedes
before the body of light and love.
All these are mere formations of the elements
making up the body.

However transient,
the body is the only temple we must visit.
For while it lives it never lies.
It dies on the pyre of truth;
it is the only shrine that holds
the fleeting eternity in us.
A river of blood and banks of bone —
the body bears witness to the ever-present
current of life.

The body grows as our idea of it grows.
In bliss it expands to fill a whole wilderness.
In sorrow the same body shrinks
like an in-growing cave.
From the infinite to the infinitesimal,

The Body

The body is a melody of five elements:
air, water, earth, fire and space.
It is the string on which
the music of the spirit is struck.

This eternal music floats in air
and vanishes in time,
only to leave behind
some fireside stories that people
remember at times.

Only true lovers know
that life stirring in their bodies —
the fugitive eyes, arrested lips
drunken limbs and two hearts on fire
quicken their voyage toward life immortal

Lovers stretch their entwined arms
to catch a silken thread
that hangs loose from the garment of One
cosmic being.

Partly of this earth and part ethereal
their bodies are oven in waking dreams

from stars to stardust,
is the journey of this body.

All ailments speak of your alienation from the light of your being;
every disease tells you of your estrangement from the ease of being.
Therefore think of your body as a prayer.
The passions that arise within
are an aspiration for the greater being.

Only true lovers know
that life stirring in their bodies —
fugitive eyes, arrested lips,
drunken limbs and hearts on fire —
quicken their voyage toward life immortal.

Lovers stretch their entwined limbs
to catch a silken thread
hanging loose from the garment of the
One cosmic being.
Partly of this earth and part ethereal,
their bodies are woven in waking dreams.

On the Senses

Sleep was broken
by flickering fireflies.
It was a night of the senses.
Mariann saw through the eyes of the night:
bodies twisting and turning
in all their wild beauty,
waiting to be possessed.
A half moon lingered like a luminous breast
behind the dark silhouette of the mountain.

Then, the priest,
whose arrogance showed
through his tattered clothes
and cultivated piety said,
What would you say about the Senses?

Ananda said,
The senses are your mind's messengers.
They stretch their arms to the wilderness of
the world
and bring news to the mind.

The senses are close kin of the elements.
Eyes open to light,
ears mate with sound,
nose breathes fragrant air,
tongue tastes water,
skin tingles with the touch of earth and fire.

Those who curse the senses,
know not that they close their doors and
windows
to their own spirit.
Senses when truly harnessed
give us a foretaste of the whole.
A pinch of salt on the tongue
makes the whole body salty.

A gentle touch of the loved one
quickens the spirit in us,
like thousand lightening streaks falling on
earth.

Our senses do not lie.
They are faithful couriers of nature's musings.

On the Senses

The sleep of the night was broken
by flickering fireflies.
It was a night of the senses.
Mariann saw through the eyes of the night
watching over bodies twisting and turning
in all their wild beauty,
waiting to be possessed.

Our senses do not lie to us.
They are faithful couriers
of nature's musings.
They say
all the elements that make the world
are within us.
They take us to the source of life
to which we long to return again and again
They teach us this secret:

The immeasurable depth of the ocean
is in us;
the high aspiring mountains are within
They whisper to us:
You are as magnificient as a bonfire
and as vast as the air you breathe.

They say all
the elements that make the world
are within us.
They take us to the source of life to which
we long to return.
They teach us this secret:
the immeasurable depth of the ocean is in us,
the high aspiring mountains are within.
They whisper to us:
you are magnificent as a bonfire
and vast as the air you breathe.

Senses are like children.
They neither know too much nor doubt
themselves.
Only the mind builds airy castles
with the gatherings of the senses
and fashions a make believe world
that vanishes like mist
before the sunshine of reality.

The mind thus limits the reality
presented by the senses

like a dusty windowpane
checking the light of dawn.

So pay attention to what the senses offer you.
And know they bring neither opinion nor
judgement,
but merely a glimpse of Truth.
It is only the mind
that distorts this face
just as a crooked mirror
curves a perfect smile
into a grimace.
Senses know what they taste,
the mind deceives by what it interprets.

Make your senses faithful servants of your
presence —
not a colony of thoughts governed by your
arrogant mind.
Let them nod their heads in harmony
with one eternal dance of Truth
that courses through your blood in rhythmic
measure.

On the Mind

Then a scholar, with his wrinkled brow and
glassy eyes said,
Tell us about the Mind.

And Ananda answered:
The mind is thought in motion.
And, being a movement
it cannot stand still.
Stillness will spell its doom.

Our mind moves in many ways.
Sometimes, it is scattered like cotton seeds.
It becomes a fluffy wave of distraction
like an apprentice archer spraying arrows in
aimless shooting.
Then, the mind gets agitated like a dust storm,
hunting with blind intensity
for an elusive prey.

Finally, as the mind goes inwards
it becomes one-pointed
and calm like the storm's eye.
This mind is a great hunter that draws in the arrow of awareness
that is housed in the eye between the eyes
and finds a target that few can see.
This third eye is the eye within eyes,
the sense within senses.
It is the eye and ear and skin of the mind.
The animal glimpses this mind through the door of instinct;
in man, it lurks within the veil of thought.

This mind, like space, can be perceived everywhere.
It is a huge canvas
on which is painted this world of illusions.
Each picture painted on the mind looks real,
yet the painter knows it is a mere reflection.

The mind goes to sleep
when the canvas is empty of paint.
When the procession of thoughts has ceased,

On the Mind

The mind is not a thing;
it is thought in motion.
And being a movement
the mind cannot stand still.
Stillness is its end.

The animal glimpses this mind through
the door of instinct.
In man it lurks within the veil of thought

This mind like space can be perceived everywhere.
It is a huge canvas
on which is painted this world of illusions.

When the procession of thoughts has ceased,
the mind wakes to another reality
... thoughts become light.

Know that the pure, radiant heart is the
house of this light.
When thought becomes the light of the
heart
the circle of reason
embraces the greater circle of love.

the mind wakes to another reality.
All of creation happens when
thoughts in the mind lose their occupation
and retreat in wonder to their silent source.
When the mind is thus illumined by its own source,
thoughts become light.
Know that the pure, radiant heart is the house of this light.
The mind merely catches its reflection on its wavy surface.

When thought becomes the light of the heart,
the circle of reason embraces
the greater circle of love.

On Woman and Man

Then the mother of a three-year-old said,
Speak to us about Woman.

Closing his eyes,
Ananda said:
A woman is the first intimation of the unborn.
In her, our desire to be born
is awakened and fulfilled.
In the womb of the unborn all desire is
consummated,
as in stillness our desire for motion is
laid to rest.

A woman is the centre of a circle
from which
the universe of belonging radiates.
This centre is the first seed of the unborn.
The centre has no substance;
it is but a mere conception from which
everything gets created.

The essence of a seed is not a substance;
yet the seed is the unseen destiny of a whole forest.
It is futile trying to know a woman.
A woman is not unknown life
but the unknowable of life.
Like life itself, a woman cannot be known;
she can be lived in and loved.
The centre of a woman is love.
Love is not matter,
but the source of all created matter.
Love does not yield itself to exterior knowledge of life,
for love is life itself and the reason for being alive.

There is no man who
did not hail from a woman.
And no man who will
not return to a woman.
In woman life turns a full circle.
Man's quest for woman is
nothing but the quest for life asleep within.

On Woman and Man

A woman is the first intimation of the unborn.
In her, our desire to be born is awakened and fulfilled.

Man is like the odd half of a pair of wings
without woman he cannot fly.

A man gives form to a woman's essence.
His fullness meets her pure emptiness.
The man is the hard striking of the bell;
the woman, the sound that permeates space.
Thus the slumbering song of life gets created.

The final goal of a woman is to
dissolve in the spacious fullness of love.
For a man this fullness comes with
understanding.
When love meets understanding,
When fulness meets spaciousness.
The secret One of the universe reveals itsel

A woman's quest for man is
only her search for life within that is eager for
expression.

The final ascent of a man
is the understanding of
the confluence of these two energy currents.
Man is like the
odd half of a pair of wings —
without woman he cannot fly.

A man gives form to a woman's essence;
his fullness meets her pure emptiness.
Man is like the hard striking of the bell;
woman, the sound permeating space.
Thus, the slumbering song of life gets created.

The final goal of a woman is to
dissolve in the spacious fullness of love.
For a man this fullness comes with
understanding.
When love meets understanding,
when fullness meets spaciousness,
the secret One of the universe reveals itself.

On Silence

Then the mother of a deaf girl
with muted sorrow in her eyes said,
Tell us about Silence.

Ananda waited for the murmur of the
eucalyptus leaves
to whisper its last secrets through the hills.

He seemed absorbed in a wordless
conversation with himself
as he said:
Silence is the womb of all that is
spoken and heard.
Silence is the flow of the river of intelligence.
Like riverbanks, words are mere interruptions
to this flow.
Silence is the unspoken truth of the universe.
Words are at best masks that embellish
the face of truth with their many devices.

The elements in the universe sing to each
other in silence.
The stars play merry-go-round
in silent motion;
the sunflower shows its face to the sun
in hushed communion;
the fish meditates wordlessly on the concert of
the deep ocean;
the silent wind caresses the spire of
the church.
The forlorn lover sitting on the edge
of the river
pines for her lost love in dumb despair.
Only numbing silence connects heart with
heart.

Silence is the golden interlude in lovers'
conversation.
It is the final quest of the wild, wise, sage.
Silence is the thirst of the parched earth for a
drop of rain.
It is the poet's desire for ultimate expression.

On Silence

ilence is the womb of all that
s spoken and heard.
ilence is the flow of the river of intelligence
Nords like the banks are
nere interruptions to this flow.

Through words, One becomes many;
In silence many returns to the One.

In silence creation happens:
The Master in us has created a house
called the universe.
Through words we knock at the door
of this house.
In silence the chest of treasure
is flung open.

Speak, but do not stand in the way
of the music of silence.
Your words are useless
without this music.

The original voice of life
is silence.
All other noises of the world are
mere echoes.

In silence words return to their essence,
just as noisy rivers merge with the ocean.
Through words, One becomes many;
in silence, many return to the One.
In silence creation happens:
the master in us
has created a house called the universe.

Through words we knock at the door of this
house.
In silence the chest of treasure is flung open.
Speak, but do not stand in the way
of the music of silence:
your words are useless without this music.

The original voice of life is silence —
all other noises of the world are mere echoes.

On Faith

Then a love-struck young woman
with hope and despair playing in her eyes,
asked,
Tell us about Faith.

Ananda spoke:
Faith is the first stirring of spring in deep
winter.
It is like the unseasonal bloom
anticipating a season of fruitfulness.
Faith is the first turning of the tide,
the hesitant promise of a trembling leaf on a
dying tree.
Faith is as old as the North Star,
and as new as a womb yearning to be
born.
Faith is as steadfast as a crystal,
yet as fleeting as the mind.
We see with the eye of faith
that which eyes do not see.

On Faith

Faith is the first stirring of
spring in deep winter
It is like the unseasonal bloom
that anticipates a season
of fruitfulness.
Faith is the first turning of the
tide;
it is the hesti hesitant promise of a
trembling leaf on a morbid
tree.
Faith is as old as
the North Star,
and as new as a
womb yearning to be born.
Faith is as steadfast as a crystal
yet as fleeting as the mind.

We see with the eyes of faith
that which eyes do not see.
Faith is the budding of reality
not yet tasted by ~~the~~ the senses

Birds fly as they have
faith in their wings.
Humans fly with the
wings of faith...

Faith is the budding of reality
not yet tasted by the senses.
Faith is like a child in fearful ecstasy
whom her father flings in the air
only to grasp her with firm hands
when she threatens to fall.

Birds fly as they have faith in their wings;
humans fly with wings of faith.
A bird is free because of its innocence;
man is free because of his faith.
Faith is the maturing of the seed of wonder
into the fruit of wisdom.
Faith is like a fragile flower
opening itself to a coaxing butterfly
and folding up before an arrogant wind.
So tread softly on the path of faith.
If you rush you may stumble
upon a stubborn rock of disbelief
or a pedestal of belief.
Faith is a virgin field that extends beyond
belief or disbelief
and transports you to the ultimate mystery of
life.

If you are out to trade,
then trade your knowledge for the mystery of faith.
This mystery is the ancestor of all knowledge.
Faith is the seed and knowledge is the flowering;
faith is the promise and knowledge its fulfilment.

On Knowledge

Then, a student bent like a hunchback
with his dusty bag of books asked,
Tell us then about Knowledge.

And Ananda said:
Knowledge is merely the notion of the real.
What is the seed but the invisible notion of life in a tree?
Self-knowledge is merely the notion of the real you.
You are just the curtain from behind which truth peeps.
You are no more than an idea planted in your head by your ancestors.
What was the form of your body
before you were born?
And what indeed was the shape of your mind
before you were conceived?
All you know about yourself is that you are a body

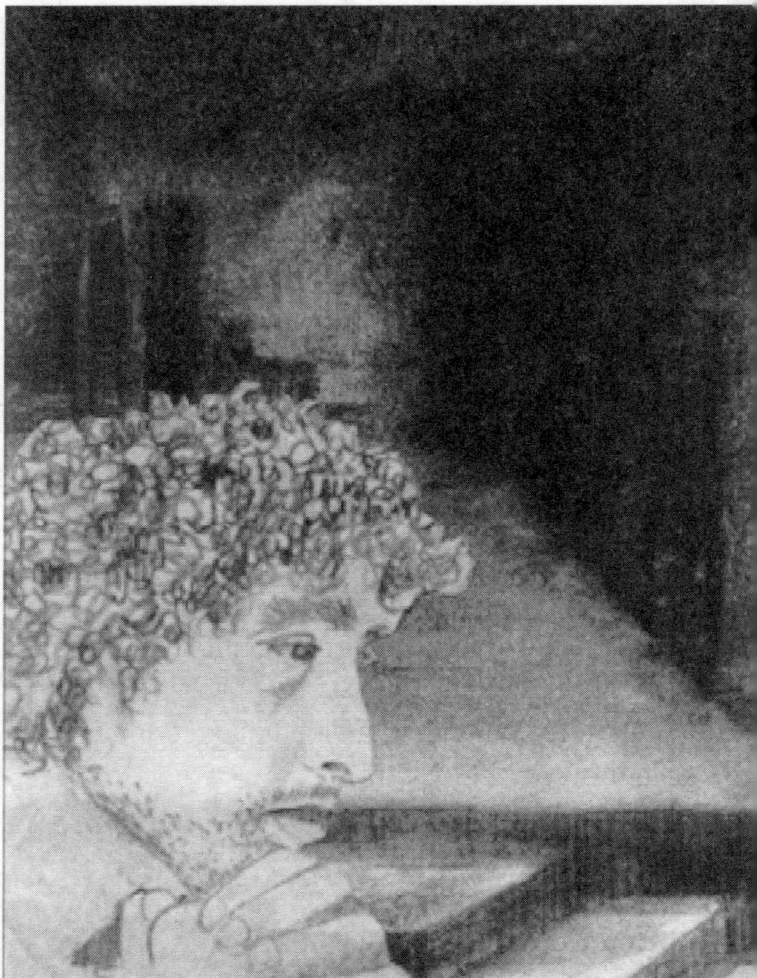

until death grinds you to the dust of a
no-body.
If you were to ask,
who was this 'I' before I was born,
you can only say:
'I was only pure knowledge that made the life
in me possible.'

Knowledge is the veil of appearance
that masks the real.
The appearance of the musk rose
is merely the knowledge of
the unseen spirit that shapes the sun and soil
into the magnificent harmony of a flower.
When your knowledge of the rose deepens
you can see the symphony of the spirit in it.
There is a magical enchantment
surrounding the petals of a rose
as it bares its heart to enraptured eyes.
That is true learning.

The knower is the one who says
I do not know.
I can only wait

On Knowledge

Knowledge is merely the notion
of the real.
What is the seed
but the invisible notion
of life in a tree?

Self-Knowledge is
merely the notion of
the real you.
You are just the curtain
from behind which truth peeps.

Those of you who scan
the horizon for a star
Know that its brilliance
stems from the
Knowledge residing
within your eyes.

You only Know
when you are Known.

Clear your eyes
so that you can
be the seer of what is true.

for the real to reveal itself.
Patience standing alone on the shore of innocence
is the only ally of learning.
Patience learns that drops make the ocean.
Patience makes the seed learn
that it is the destiny of the tree;
it makes a child
the true father of the man.
Through patience the knowing mind
comes to grips with the mystery of things.

True knowledge is not in the objects you see.
Those of you who scan the horizon for a star
know that its brilliance
stems from the knowledge residing within your eyes.

You only know
when you are known.
Knowledge is in the light in your eyes.
Lest you obscure this light with partiality or prejudice,

keep your eyes open to these two enemies of
knowledge.
Even a speck of dust in the eye of the knower
can obscure a whole universe of Truth.
Clear your eyes
so that you can be the seer of what is true.

On Freedom

A solitary old man with eyes on the setting sun then asked,
Tell us about Freedom.

Ananda answered:
Freedom is in that which does not limit our spirit.
The prisoner seeks freedom beyond the prison walls,
the diseased in health.

The first cry of freedom craves for more;
the final song of freedom desires nothing.
In between, the spirit in us struggles to be born.

Our law of being drags us through the world of many desires.
Each want fulfilled
leaves behind a hollow trail of success.
And when we return to the source at the end of our life

On Freedom

The first cry of freedom is in craving
for more.
The final song of freedom is in desiring
nothing.
In between the spirit in us struggles
to be born.

The freedom we cannot share binds us.
Lighten your burden
and go on this voyage of freedom
unattended and alone.
Even as the joy of living for others makes
our spirit lighter
freedom ~~is~~ is in ~~carrying~~ giving.
without carrying the burden of being the giver

For every pompous giver is bound by the
expectation of a reward.
This makes their gifts tainted at the source

So give in a way that makes you grateful
that there is a receiver for your gift
All that is not given away thus is lost to us
forever.
In freedom one must give the world away.
Then the world* becomes one's own.

we must travel back through the same street of
desire
picking up bits and pieces of memory
to make way for our freedom.
So that when we return one day to where we
came from
we know what we surrendered.

The freedom we cannot share binds us.
Lighten your burden
and go on this voyage of freedom unattended
and alone.
Even as the joy of living for others makes our
spirit lighter,
freedom is in giving without carrying the
burden of being the giver.
For every pompous giver is bound by the
expectation of a reward.
This makes our gifts tainted at the source.
So give in a way that makes you grateful
that there
is a receiver for your gift.

All that is not given away thus is lost to us
forever.

In freedom one must give the world away.
Then the world becomes one's own.
To be absolutely free is to receive the bounty
of the invisible giver —
clouds flowing freely like white sails
swell with the wind's charity
and unleash their wealth of rain
on the thirsty earth.

For those of you riding a tide of desire
just shift the flow of this tide from receiving to
giving.
Do you not see the sacrificial lamb fed and
fattened
before it is slaughtered by its owner?
As you take without giving,
Nature, your owner, fattens you with
unconsummated desire,
robs you of your will to be free.
You are like that deluded mason who fashions
a house
from within, furnishes it, but forgets to build
the door.

On Pain and Pleasure

Then a woman of ill repute,
her downcast eyes
hidden away from other eyes, asked,
What about Pain and Pleasure?

Ananda said:
Pain and pleasure are like the valley and peak
of a hill —
there is pain in climbing up
and pleasure in coming down.
We pay the price for climbing with our pain;
we get the reward for coming downhill with
our pleasure.
Traversing the circle of pleasure and pain
like an ox going round a mill,
is the journey of your life.

There is much pleasure when man meets
woman,

when skin rubs on skin.
The joy in us is caged within our body.
Yet this moment's delight in togetherness
is shattered by the lull of loss when,
exhausted by the mind's feverishness,
this joy gets dulled and dead in our bodies.

Pain and pleasure are companions
although they wear different masks.
Pleasure is an illusory escape from pain
like the deluded bird in flight that escapes
the valley
only to rest its tired wings in the earthly grave.
Pain seems as alien to pleasure as smoke to fire.
Yet we know that smoke without fire is a
grand delusion.

When you seek pleasure
look for the knowledge contained in it.
Surely the bud that seeks to burst into a flower
must know that it must endure the pain of
breaking its own form.
When in pain,
remember that you are merely creating
the capacity to enjoy pleasure.
The pleasure in rest is magnified by a hard
day's toil.

Watch the rise and fall of pain and pleasure
like the ebb and tide of the sea —
they are our means of existence.

On Pain and Pleasure

Pain and pleasure are companions
of each other
although they wear different masks.
Pleasure looks like an escape
from pain.
Like the bird in flight is
deluded that it escapes the valley
only to rest its tired wings in the earthly
grave.
Pain seems as alien to pleasure
as smoke to fire.
Yet we know that smoke without fire
is a grand delusion.

Watch the rising and falling of the scales
of pleasure and pain.
When a jeweller weighs his gold
has his eyes fixed in the ~~middle~~ middle
of the scale
until two scales become equal.

Be a firm witness to pleasure and pain
and know that in the quiet, still centre
of your watchfulness
both pleasure and pain are equalised.

Give pleasure even when you are in pain:
does not the singer create
the most mellifluous tune
from the depths of despondency?

See in your pain the threshold of pleasure
like a mother in labour aches for the joy of
renewed life.
What is pain but the craving for lost pleasure!
Watch the rising and falling of the scales of
pleasure and pain,
just as a jeweller does when weighing his
gold —
he has his eyes fixed in the middle
until the two scales become equal.
Be a firm witness to pleasure and pain
and know that in the quiet, still centre of your
watchfulness
both pleasure and pain are equalised.

The Face of Truth

Then a woman with veiled eyes, asked,
What does Truth look like?

Ananda said:
Truth is naked.
You cannot embrace it,
until your mind is stripped of all its fancies.
If you cannot do that
at least take off some of your clothes
so that you become lighter for the journey.

Truth lives in us,
but is faceless.
Truth has many facades,
but not a single face.

Seeking the face of Truth is like looking for the face of light.

In light all things are seen,
but why does light never show itself?
Have you ever thought that you are the light
shining through the truth of your being.
What if we know we are that light itself?
What a pity when we look for what we
already are.

Truth is reflected in many faces.
The beehive is a maze of mansions,
and yet the honey that flows though them is
all one.
When crushed to its very essence
the hive is one sweet stream of honey
So is the nature of Truth in many bodies.
Under the jaws of death we become one with
our essence.

Truth is a mirror of the infinite.
Before its steadfast gaze
every other face is a mere procession of the
finite.
We are but living statues.
When our faces wither away like autumn

The Face of Truth

Truth is naked.
You cannot embrace it,
until your mind is stripped of all
its fancy dressing.
If you cannot do that
at least take off some of your clothes
so that you become lighter for
the journey.

Truth lives in all of us.
But is faceless.
Truth has many facades
but not a single face.

Seeking the face of Truth is like
looking for the face of light.
In light all things are seen
Why does light never show itself?
In Truth all things are established.
But Truth is never seen in its shrine.

Truth is reflected in many faces
The beehive is a maze of mansions
Yet, the honey that flows through them is all one
When crushed to its very essence the hive
is one sweet stream of honey.
So is the nature of Truth in many bodies.

leaves,
what remains is faceless Truth.

The woman then asked,
If Truth has no face how do you recognise it?

Ananda placed his palm on his heart and said:
To know Truth from falsehood
look into your heart,
for Truth has a deep kinship with it.

Falsehood is a device of the crafty.
A crafty mind cannot see the truth a pure heart perceives.
The mind swarming with thoughts cannot see past its own veil.
Of what use is a looking glass in the conference of the blind?

Falsehood stirs the heart while truth stills it.
Therefore truth is best reflected in a heart that is tranquil.
In truth the heart becomes the door to all the riches of the world.

The Creator cannot live His life without you
for His heart is expressed through yours.
He cannot speak without your voice.
So live every moment of your life in the
ecstasy of His creation,
utter every word as though
it was His voice of truth.
You will then catch a glimpse of the real.

On Sexuality

Mariann's face was flushed with longing,
her eyes restless as a startled deer.
Desire crept up her spine in waves of ecstasy.
She watched a pair of lovers in the distance
cling like tender vines.
He plundering her beauty like an imperious
king,
she squandering kisses in reckless
abandon —
two bodies, one spirit.

Ananda held Mariann in an embrace
that seemed to her like frozen eternity.
She felt the whole universe beside her.
It was as though the entire song of creation
was ringing through her.
She asked, her face now simmering with numb
wanting,
Tell us about the fulfilment of Desire.

Ananda spoke in an unwavering voice:
Desire and its fulfilment are inseparable from one another,
like fire and its flame.
Fire is passionate but blind,
and the flame lends to fire its luminous eyes.
True to its nature, fire consumes everything in its reckless abandon

and leaves behind cold ashes of memory.
When a fire is tamed by self-sacrifice,
the flame of desire rises in aspiration.

In aspiration,
man and woman seek liberation from their forms.
Like an overflowing cup
they share their abundance, not their hunger for each other.
Making love is a call to break the loneliness
of limiting bodies to find
the solitude of shared bliss.

Lovemaking — caressing of skins,
rubbing of liquid lips and flammable flesh —
creates occasional sparks
but does not quench the lifelong thirst for completion.

The sheath of the body
is like the shell of a coconut.
It covers the desire-free fruit of ecstasy
that never clings to its shell.

The longing of this body is
to attain the fruitfulness of desire in
desirelessness.

Lovemaking is Nature's play for unveiling
a human being's dark sacredness
into the light of awareness.
Lovers weave their bodies
into one magical tapestry.
In this tapestry hides the silken thread of the
sacred.
This thread thickens into awareness,
and through awareness lovers can lift their
bodies
into one bodiless being.

Women and men bind each other in
unattainable longing —
voluptuous bodies simmer and spin,
tender breasts cuddle against taut skin,
sparks flow like darts from arched eyes.
What a blooming jasmine does
to a drunken bee,
or the wild west wind to a mulberry tree —

On Sexuality

Desire and its fulfilment are
two aspects of the same thing,
like fire and its flame.
One is inseparable from the other.
Fire is passionate but blind,
and the flame lends to fire its luminous eyes.
True to its nature, fire consumes everything
in its reckless abandon
and leaves behind cold ashes of memory.
When a fire is tamed by self-sacrifice,
the flame of desire rises in aspiration.

In aspiration,
man and woman seek liberation ~~f~~ from
their forms.
Like an overflowing cup
they share their abundance, not their
hunger for each other.

Lovemaking is discovering the spirit
in the flesh.
From this communion is born
a community.
It is the sacred search of the One
for its own multitude.

the physical forms of man and woman
attract each other.
Yet, it is the same form that acts as a
barrier to the unity of their being.

Therefore, in your passionate embrace
don't cling merely
to the appetite of your body.
Give joy away; surrender to your otherness —
you will reap your reward in utter ecstasy.

Make the body a prayer.
Roll all your desires into one
giant wave of aspiration
that will lash on the shores of freedom.
Let the urge to merge into one being
reveal to you
the One that resides within two bodies.
Lovemaking is discovering the spirit in the flesh.
From this communion is born a community.
It is the sacred search of the One for its
own multitude.

On Intimacy

The lovers cuddled —
arm locked in arm,
eyes nestled in eyes.
They were close together
yet with a thirst of wilderness in them.
The liquid moon stole an occasional glance
through the curtain of leaves.
They asked, Tell us about Intimacy.

Ananda looked adoringly towards them and said:
We live in the world of the form and the formless.
To be intimate is to dissolve the form into the formless.

A cube of ice rolls over and glides
gently into a pool of water.
The form of ice becomes intimate with

formless water.
The ice surrenders its form;
yet its presence remains in the coolness of the water.

To be intimate you must learn to forget
your little selves
and merge in the service of the Self that resides in both of you.
In One Self the desires of two are fulfilled.
Earn your pleasure by pleasuring the other;
find your own bliss by making the other blissful;
breathe together so that you can become one breath.

Let your hearts beat in one harmonious rhythm.
Let that one lyric of spring linger on your sealed lips.

In abandoning our self we can truly be intimate.
In letting go we find our goal of togetherness.

On Intimacy

o be intimate is to dissolve the form
nto the formless.

A cube of ice rolls over and glides
gently into a pool of water.
he form of ice has now become intimate
with formless water.
The ice surrenders its form;
yet its presence remains in the coolness
of the water.

Intimacy is what remains when we
are no longer close ~~togethe~~ together
n our bodies.
et we bond with our spirits.

There is a longing in us
that goes beyond the fire in our flesh.
Intimacy is the longing of that One Self
in us
to merge with its own expression.

The flickering passion of a matchstick
stands out in the dark of the night.
But does this light not vanish
before the blazing white sun?

We are most intimate when we are most carefree.

Intimacy is what remains when we are no longer
close together through our physical forms.
Yet we bond with our spirits.
There is a longing in us
that goes beyond the fire in our flesh.

Intimacy is the longing of that One Self in us
to merge with its own expression.
The flickering passion of a matchstick
stands out in the dark of the night.
But does this light not vanish
before the blazing white sun?

On Giving and Taking

Mariann held Ananda's hand and said,
Speak to us about Giving and Taking.

Ananda answered:
What is not given is lost forever.
For the one who gives not
holds water with a fishnet.
This universe is one grand design of giving.
The tree gives fruit, the soil fertility;
the water in the river quickens the life in you;
the stars with their celestial symphony go
around you everyday;
the wind waits in hushed stillness to listen to
your laughter.

Then looking at Mariann he said:
Your dress looks purple for it holds back
all the colours but purple.

It is thus known by whatever it gives away to
the world.
As the sunflower is known
by the bright radiance it offers to the sun,
and the wild rose by the heady fragrance
it gives away to the forest.
In giving, you empty your storehouse of riches,
but that emptiness is where all the riches lie.
The emptiness
of a burning candle is the source of light,
of a house is the comfort it provides,
of non-existence is the source of all
existence.

You give only to take the fullness of non-
existence.
All the bounties of the world are in the womb
of this non-existence.
Therefore take as you give.
As you give, you take the capacity to give
from the One.
The sun empties its light in a million rays
and yet shines with all its glory day after day.

On Giving and Taking

What is not given is lost for ever.
For the one who gives not
holds water with a fishnet.

The universe is one grand design of giving
The tree gives fruit, the soil fertility.
The water in the river quickens the life in
you.
The stars in their celestial symphony go
around you everyday.
The wind waits in hushed stillness
to listen to your laughter.
Then looking at Mariann he said,
You are what you give.

You give only to take the fullness of non-existence
All the bounties of the world are in the womb
of this non-existence.
Therefore take as you give.
As you give you take the capacity to give from
the One.

Giving and taking are two channels
of one flowing spirit.
That which goes from The One
comes back to its source.

Giving and taking are two channels of the one flowing spirit.
That which goes from the One comes back to the source.
So give with the abundance of an ocean tide
and all the riches of the world
will roll back on you.
Give until your body becomes a burning candle
and your resisting mind turns to ashes.
You will create One great light.
And when you light a million candles from that one source of light,
the original flame will still burn undiminished.
Such is the law of the spirit.

On Nature

Mariann looked at the sun poised on the temple-top,
a bewitching arc of light.
The sky wore an unspeakable allure of colours.
Her eyes swept a garden of flowers:
a cluster of marigolds closeted together
like close friends caught her eyes.
She turned to Ananda and said,
Speak to me about Nature.

Ananda looked quietly into the receding light
mellowed red in its parting hour,
and said:
Nature is a play of many shapes and forms
born of the joy of emptiness.
The morning glory blooms and fades.
All things in nature live and grow out of sheer ecstasy.

Emptiness is at the heart of this ecstasy.
Voiceless bamboo can become
the flute of divine music
only when it is empty of itself.
A boat full of water sinks without a trace.
The same boat resurrects like a graceful swan
when it is empty.
The fragrance of a musk rose cannot be
caught;
it lives in its formless presence in the wild.
All of Nature scribble their script on the face
of emptiness.
The sky is an open invitation to experience
the freedom of the formless.
The infinite grace that shapes the majesty of
the sky
also embraces us.
The sky speaks to us in the glittering language
of the stars —
the message of our omnipresence.

Mountains teach us detachment —
to behold their greatness we must stand away
from them.

On Nature

Nature is a play of many shapes and forms
born of the joy of emptiness.
The morning glory blooms, furls, unfurls
and fades away.
All things in nature live and grow
out of utter ecstasy.

Emptiness is at the heart of this ecstasy.
The hollow bamboo can become
the flute of divine music
only when it is empty of itself.

All of Nature scribble their script
on the face of emptiness.
The sky is an open invitation
to experience the freedom of the formless
The infinite grace that shapes
the majesty of the sky
also embraces us.
The sky speaks to us
in the glittering language
of the stars
the message of our omnipresence.

The enigma of the hills is the lure
of the unconquered aspects of our selves.
The rocks are foundations of truth — ageless.
Turn a stone —
you will find fossils of your hoary ancestors.
Pluck a flower in full bloom —
you will see your youth there.
The running water in the rocks is a clear
stream of reason
cutting through the moss of ignorance.
Taste that water and you will
drink the fountain of knowledge.

The wind leaves its graffiti everywhere —
touching the silken surface of sand,
murmuring through dried leaves,
inscribing its sonnet on the soil.
If you listen to the wind
you will hear your soul's wanderlust.

The desire in you wills
and the nature in you creates.
Nature's first impulse is to create.

Man and woman are held together
in nature's invisible thread of creation.
Together, they bring will and desire
into one flowing fountain of ecstasy.

On Beauty

The golden garment of the evening was
caught in a noose of light.
Rapt in the spell of the moment,
the wonder-struck poetess came forward.

She asked, Tell us about Beauty.
Ananda saw the receding light
kissing silken leaves in the far horizon.
His face was now swathed in crimson glow.

He said:
Beauty is a symphony of the senses
born of a harmony with the whole.

Beauty is in the magic stirring in your heart
and in the measure shaping your mind.
It is in the mystery delighting your soul.

Beauty comes from the unity of senses
when the knot of desire is loosened

On Beauty

Beauty is a symphony of the senses
born of a harmony with the whole.

Beauty is in the magic that stirs in your hear
and in the measure that shapes your mind
It is in the mystery that delights your soul.

Beauty comes from the unity of the senses.
When the knot of desire is loosened
and lips pout in their liquid lustre.
When flesh devours flesh
and impatient kisses leave
their rude signature on a fair face.
The lover's eyes become flames
made of flesh.

When two beautiful bodies meet,
they find their rhythm with universal
harmonies.
It is only with the open heart
one can see this harmony.

Doors open behind doors
And senses behind senses.
The essence of this beauty is timeless.

and lips pout in liquid lustre.
When flesh devours flesh
and impatient kisses leave their rude
signature on a fair face,
the lovers' eyes become flames made of flesh.

When two beautiful bodies meet,
they find their rhythm in universal harmony.
It is only with an open heart that this
harmony can be seen.
You too can hear this rhythm with your eyes
closed.
The dazzling face of beauty hides the subtler
harmony of truth.

When you knock on the sleepy doors of your
senses
you awaken to the world of the real.
Doors open behind doors
and senses behind senses.
The essence of this beauty is timeless.
It is only in time that this essence takes shape
and form.
Beauty is the eternal hunger of your soul
to witness its own reflection in Nature.

This hunger gives us the eye to behold and the tongue to savour
the magnificence of the soul's unity with all.
Like a glittering diamond, beauty has many faces.
But who can see this beauty
until the diamond lets the light of the One shine through it?

On Love and Fear

A wizened old man clutching the hands of his grandson, then said,
Tell us about Love and Fear.

And Ananda answered:
We are the light of love.
Fear is love with a mask.
The lover fears the loss of the beloved.
For where is this fear if there is no love
between the two?

It is because of the grand fear
of love's eternal laws
that planets move in their orbits;
seasons shift in inexorable cycles.
The sun shines,
the moon waxes and wanes,
and the sea ebbs and flows.

Behind the mask of this grand fear lies
the grander design of love.
If you look with fearful eyes
the world would seem apart from you
like the yawning chasm of a stiff mountain.
If you look through the heart of love
you will behold a safe and supporting valley.
Crushed grapes shrink from each other in fear
only to flow together
in the distilled wine of love.

In the heart of love
you are one
with the flying birds;
the swiftly moving fish;
the babble of breeze breaking the vast
solitude of the forest.
You cannot describe what shape your love
takes,
for like a dancing leaf gone with the wind
you are no longer there.

In the web of love
the farthest draws near,

On Love and Fear

Ananda said,
We are the light of love.
Fear is love with a mask.
The lover fears the loss of the beloved.
There is fear when indivisible love is divided
between the two.

It is because of the grand fear
of love's eternal laws
that ~~pla~~ planets move in their orbits;
seasons shift in inexorable cycles.
The sun shines,
The moon waxes ~~or~~ and wanes.
And the sea ebbs and flows.

Behind the mask of this grand fear
lies the grander design of love

Fear grows out of the moss of ignorance
that gathers around the sparkling
water of love.
Look behind the moss and you will find
love's ~~interrupted~~ uninterrupted flow.

Love accepts fear as the distortion
of its own nature.
Just as light embraces darkness
as its own absence.

the alien grows dear.
To be in love is to be established in your own nature.
To fear is to lose touch with your inborn wholeness.

Fear grows out of the moss of ignorance
gathering around the sparkling water of love.
Look behind the moss and you will find
love's uninterrupted flow.
Love accepts fear as the distortion of its own nature,
just as light embraces darkness as its own absence.

On Death

Then a rickety old man with sunken eyes
asked,
Tell us now of Death.

And Ananda said:
Our life is a boisterous bubble
rising from the silent sea of death.
Like a house of mirrors
life is a many-splendoured illusion.

Both life and death
are extensions of each other —
living on like the rising and falling of our
breathing.
Even as you indulge in life's feast
be prepared to fast on death's bed.
And with a serene mind go home to rest,
for life will beckon you again
for another journey.

Learn to die to your desires
if you want them fulfilled.
Bury them like seeds in the soil —
one day they will sprout in a burst of
abundance.
The soil does not reveal the secrets of life
until the seed learns to die to its form.
Death of the fleeting forms of flowers yields to

fruitfulness;
the child form must die before youth makes its appearance.
The grain of corn must perish to its form
before it can multiply.

Like music, life needs a terminal point.
It is from the silence between notes
that music draws its breath.
Death is the undertone that supports life's tone.
Death and life intermingling
form an inseparable unity.

The world's a passing spectacle,
and one human life
less than a wink in life's grand carnival.
Yet that little wink can hold the vision of eternity
to one who is fully awake.

Live as though you will die to your body
in the very next instant.
Search behind the ashes of your body,

you will find the undying spirit
like a long lost treasure.
Begin your courtship with this spirit.
It will give you wings to travel far.

Life eternal is granted to the one
who even as he is in the world
has learnt to die to it.
For what is death
but the mirror reflecting the fleeting beauty of the world.

Do not see Death like a shadow
casting its gloom by
obscuring the light of life.
Let death watch even as life sleeps.
In this watching, life will be a joy and a celebration.

Death eavesdrops through the veil of appearance
and raises its banner of everlasting life
through the procession of frail mortality.
Die, so that you are born every moment.

On Death

fe is a boisterous ~~bubble~~ bubble
ising from the silent sea of death.
ike a house of mirrors
ife is a many splendoured illusion
f appearances.

oth life and death
re extensions of each other,
iving on like the rising and falling
f our breathing.

ven as you indulge in life's feast
e prepared to fast on death's bed.
nd with a serene mind prepare to rest.

he world's a passing spectacle
and the one human life less than a wink
n Life's grand carnival.
Yet that little wink can hold the vision
of eternity to the one who is fully awake.

Death eavesdrops through the veil of appearance
and raises its banner of everlasting life
through the procession of frail mortality.
Die, so that you are born every moment.

For death hides in its depth life's most enduring secret,
as a frail seed writes in dust the vision of a forest.

The Parting

The hour of parting drew near.
The air was empty of all music
like the streets of a deserted city.
Not a leaf stirred.
The ghostly palm trees lay
drowsing in the slow breeze
like many sleep-worn bodies.

Tears swelled in Mariann's eyes
leaden with the burden of separation.
She sat sad and solemn —
the cry of a bird that has lost sight of its nest.
Mariann thought
the vast, solitary twilight will become
even more sad without Ananda.

The indigo curtain of
the night lay in ambush.
The last leisurely shadows

of a tired and tardy sun
crept over the top of the temple.
The farewell hour tiptoed in hushed
expectancy.

Mariann, in a voice quivering with sorrow, said,
When you are not there, Ananda,
the wind will freeze to a sullen sonata,
and the city's noise will drown in a deep
sadness.

When you are not there
the sunflowers on my terrace
will look away —
cold and forsaken
as though all poetry has faded from them.

When you are not there
a confused kite will wobble in the sky
unsure which way the wind will blow.
Curtains will drop like heavy eyelids
on foggy windowpanes:
the day will end,
and you will not be there.

The Parting

ears swelled in Mariann's eyes
eaden with the burden of separation.
he sat sad and solemn ~~like~~ —
a cry of a bird that had
ost sight of its nest.

Mariann thought, the vast solitary twilight
will become still more sad without
Ananda.

Mariann with a voice ~~quiet~~ quivering
with sorrow said:
When you are not there Ananda,
the wind will freeze to a sullen sonata
and the city's noise would drown
in a deep, still sadness.

When you are not there
the sunflowers on my terrace
will look away — cold and forsaken
as though all poetry has
~~fa~~ faded from them.

When you are not there
a confused kite would wobble in the sky
unsure which way the wind shall blow.

A solitary sparrow will look over the balcony
when you are not there,
looking like a river without ripples
mourning in the sunset.

When you are not there,
I would still hear your footfall
in the wilderness.
Leaves will crackle under my feet.
Will fallen leaves, like memories
still whisper your voice when you are gone?

Ananda said:
Like the spring I shall visit you
in the buzzing of drunken bees
and the blossoming of mango trees
heavy with fruitfulness.

When winter arrives
I shall be in the spotless
beauty of snow
and in the austerity of tender trees
shorn of foliage.

I shall be in a falling leaf and in a fluttering butterfly.
For, I am the One connecting the earth and the sky
living beyond birth and decay.

I shall come again in
a child's merrymaking
and an old man's toothless grin.

Then he looked at the river in tide.
His eyes reflected the many faces of the flowing water.

Learn from this river
that life is one beginning-less flow
and we are nowhere in form but everywhere in this flow.
The ebbs and tides are but brief sojourns
like many livings and dyings.

I shall visit you again in wings of love
floating in the music of the hummingbird.
I shall be there in the first gasp of a new born life

and in the last prayer from the old, worn mosque.
For, I am the life coursing through the universe
in one eternal circle of love.

The mist was now lifted by
a million luminous strings of sunrays.

Ananda said:
Farewell my friend!
What I have given you
is all that I have received
from the abundant life we share.
Remember to love this life in all forms and shapes,
for you will then be a true servant of our love.

I shall live forever in your love.
Saying this, Ananda melted into the river
like a swift flowing stream.

Mariann felt the stream in her tears
trickling down her trembling lips.

She heard her own voice murmuring,
Farewell my friend!
My heart knows you will return
in the dream of every woman
aching with youth.
You will visit every devout man
bent in prayer.

I know you will come back again with the
rising of the next tide.
For you are that love we seek,
and you hide.

Until then, farewell.